Osborne

Michael Turner, MVO

CONTENTS

Tour of the House 3
Exterior 3
Grand Corridor 4
Council Room 5
Audience Room 6
Grand Corridor (continued) 6
Table-deckers' Rooms 8
Dining Room 8
Drawing Room 9
Billiard Room 11
Nursery 12
Staircase 14
Pages' Alcove 14
Prince Albert's Bathroom 15
Prince Albert's Dressing
and Writing Room 15
Queen Victoria's
Sitting Room 17
Queen Victoria's
Dressing Room 18
Queen Victoria's
Bedroom 18
Horn Room 21
Queen Victoria's Lift 21
Durbar Corridor 23
Durbar Room 24

Tour of the Gardens 26
Terraces 26
Walled Garden and
Pleasure Grounds 28
Swiss Cottage Garden 30
Swiss Cottage 31
Swiss Cottage Museum 34
Victoria Fort and
Albert Barracks 34
Osborne Beach 35

History 37

Special Features
Birthdays at Osborne 20
Queen Victoria and India 22
John Brown 29
The Royal Family Tree 43
The Royal Children 44
The Convalescent Home 51
A Maid at Osborne 52

Plans
The Pavilion 7
Site plans   inside back cover

Tour of the House

Osborne was built as a family home by the sea rather than a palace, and the Pavilion at the heart of the house is an embodiment of Victorian family values. Lived in for only 55 years, the house is a unique evocation of the private tastes and ambitions of Queen Victoria and Prince Albert, and a vivid and touching recreation of royal daily life at both domestic and court level.

EXTERIOR

The household wing, the southern part of the house, accommodated members of the royal household, offices and guests. It was completed in 1851 by the building contractor Thomas Cubitt (1788–1855) of London, as was the main wing to its rear, and is built of brick with a cement render coloured to resemble stone.

The mahogany window frames were painted in Victoria's lifetime to protect the wood. At first-floor level are four cement copies of classical statues. These were commercially available and demonstrate Albert's desire to clothe Osborne with classical respectability, but at a cost to suit the queen's privy purse.

On the far right is a small attached building whose only entrance is the outside door. This is

the smoking room, built in 1866 for the Prince of Wales because the queen would not tolerate smoking in the house. It is not open to the public. To the left of the household wing is the carriage ring. The iron lamps supported by dolphins are a reminder that Osborne was a seaside home.

The Grand Corridor is on the right. Above, the arcade of Ionic Venetian windows was inspired by Andrea Palladio's arcading to the basilica at Vicenza (built 1549–1614). The arcade gave access from the Pavilion to the elder children's rooms in the main wing, which overlooks the terraces and Osborne Beach. A glazed passage between the Pavilion and the main wing was added in 1877.

The central block is the Pavilion, the first part of Osborne built by Cubitt, in 1846. It housed the family's private apartments. The only extensive use of real stone on the exterior is the Portland stone porte cochère, where travellers could alight from a carriage under cover.

Left of the Pavilion is the Durbar wing, designed in 1890 by John Randall Mann (1828–1918), who served his apprenticeship with Cubitt and had been surveyor of works at Osborne since 1857. Unlike its interior, its façades are conservative, to blend with the Italianate style of the main house.

Above: The carriage ring, with the Grand Corridor behind. The cement basket in the centre was first planted with heather by Prince Albert in 1849

Below: The Calydonian boar at the entrance to the household wing. This modern stone sculpture copies the original destroyed in 1918

Facing page: Detail of the embossed wallpaper below the gallery of the Durbar Room

Household Wing and Main Wing

The steps up to the household wing are flanked by copies of the Calydonian boar on the left and the dog of Alcibiades on the right. The dog is the original cement copy by the London artificial-stone manufacturer Austin & Seeley. An introductory exhibition is located in what was the household dining room. The plaster cornice depicting grapes recalls its original function.

▮ GRAND CORRIDOR

This corridor links the household and main wings, and Victoria's private apartments. The decoration (largely repainted in the 1980s) was devised, with Ludwig Gruner, by Albert, and reflects his liking for Italian Renaissance design. High on the walls are small plaster copies of friezes from the Parthenon,

modelled and supplied by the sculptor John Henning (1771–1851) in 1846. The corridor was designed to resemble a classical sculpture gallery common in late 18th- and 19th-century country houses. Here, however, most of the sculptures were by living British and European artists.

Unlike other royal residences, Osborne was lived in for only 55 years and so clearly shows the tastes of Victoria and Albert, the sole builders of the collection. In many ways it is Albert's creation. After his death in 1861 the queen added to the collection but did not alter significantly the prince's arrangement of it. Her additions were perhaps less scholarly and more sentimental in character.

The ebonized cabinets are part of the 1850s decorative scheme. The bronzes on top of them are mostly reduced copies of antique figures and popular works. Halfway down the corridor in a gilded niche is a statue of Victoria in classical costume by John Gibson (1790–1866). The queen gave it to Albert for his birthday in 1849. In front

Ground floor

of the statue sections of the Minton tile floor are exposed. The design includes the arms of Great Britain and maritime symbols. The main wing to the right housed principal guests, and the royal children when they left the nursery. The corridor on the ground floor is not restored, so the varnish on the marbled pilasters has yellowed with age.

2 COUNCIL ROOM

Here the queen's privy council of ministers met several times a year, and in this room in June 1857 the queen gave Albert the title 'Prince Consort'. It is the most elaborately decorated room at Osborne. The colour scheme, settled by Gruner and Albert, was completed in 1859. The room was also used for entertaining – dancing, charades and drama. In the centre of the ceiling is the badge of the Order of the Garter and other royal emblems. As in most of the fine rooms at Osborne, the original paint survives in the picking-out of ceiling elements, whereas the larger areas of plain colour on the ceiling and walls have been over-painted.

The door through which visitors enter is flanked by portraits on Sèvres porcelain of Victoria and Albert that were presented by Louis Philippe, King of France, in 1846. The painting *The Deer Drive* on the end wall is a Victorian copy of the original intended for this room by Sir Edwin Landseer (1802–73). French windows lead on to the upper terrace.

On 14 January 1878 in this room Alexander Graham Bell demonstrated his telephone, which had been patented for less than two years. 'It is rather faint and one must hold the tube rather close to one's ear,' commented the queen, but

telephones were nevertheless installed in 1885. A lift outside was installed for the convalescent home in what was an alcove giving light to the corridor, where ministers waited to attend a meeting. The convalescent home used the room for smoking, hence the severe yellowing of the ceiling. Photographs of the 19th century show the silk chenille carpet by Templeton's of Glasgow dated mdcccli (1851); it was displayed in Albert's Great Exhibition that year and bought by Victoria, who had it adapted to fit. It remained at Osborne until the 1920s, when it went to the British embassy in Washington DC. It later went to the Smithsonian Institution, which generously presented the carpet to English Heritage in 1988 for redisplay.

Over the doors on each side of the marble chimneypiece are pediments containing medallions of Albert and Victoria supported by Roman gods and goddesses added in 1855 by William Theed (1804–91), Queen Victoria's favourite sculptor. The left-hand door leads to the audience room.

Left: The council room set for a privy council meeting in about 1857. The plain ceiling and doors were elaborately redecorated in 1859
Below: The council room, showing the Templeton's carpet

Ground floor

3 AUDIENCE ROOM

Queen Victoria frequently received ministers here before privy council meetings. Holland & Sons supplied the original furniture in 1851 and much of it survives, including the writing table and gilt satinwood chairs upholstered in crimson damask. The remarkable coloured glass and ormolu (gilt brass) chandelier represents convolvulus (Albert's favourite flower) and arum lilies climbing out of a basket. It was probably manufactured in Berlin.

1 GRAND CORRIDOR (CONTINUED)

The queen took exercise here on the rare occasions when bad weather stopped her going out. The white and gold candelabra with two-burner lamps and bird's-beak benches with morocco-leather seats form part of the original furniture.

A grey marble statue on the left is of Antinous, Emperor Hadrian's favourite page, who was drowned in the Nile in AD 122. It was thought to be Egypto-Roman when it was sold at Northwood Park, Cowes, in 1850, but is now believed to be a

Right: The audience room. The chandelier represents convolvulus, Prince Albert's favourite flower. The oil painting, Christ in the Temple, *by Marie Ellenrieder, was bought by Albert in 1849*
Below: The statue of Noble, Victoria's collie, by Sir Joseph Edgar Boehm (1834–90)

19th-century copy of a statue in the Vatican. The white marble statue is a winged Victory by C D Rauch (1777–1857).

The corridor turns left. Near the end is a bay window and the opposite wall contains an inset panel by John Gibson of Cupid and Psyche, who swore eternal love for each other and with whom the royal couple identified themselves.

Beyond, the main entrance hall to the Pavilion is painted in imitation of grey marble. The mahogany side table, cupboard and chairs are typical of austere early-Victorian hall furniture.

The Pavilion

Cubitt completed the Pavilion in 1845. In the design of the inside he was influenced by a London Georgian townhouse plan.

The basement houses service rooms, including a boiler room with the necessary coal cellars underneath the carriage ring (not open to the public). At ground-floor level are the principal rooms. They envelop a spacious full-height staircase hall, but the arrangement of a suite of salons – the dining room leading into the drawing room, which in turn leads into the billiard room – is more Continental in style. It suggests the influence of Prince Albert's German background.

The couple's most intimate rooms are on the first floor, with Albert's domain on the right and Queen Victoria's on the left, meeting in the shared sitting room in the centre.

The nurseries and servants' rooms are on the second floor. The 32.6m tall flag tower contains an observation room reached by a spiral staircase (not open to the public).

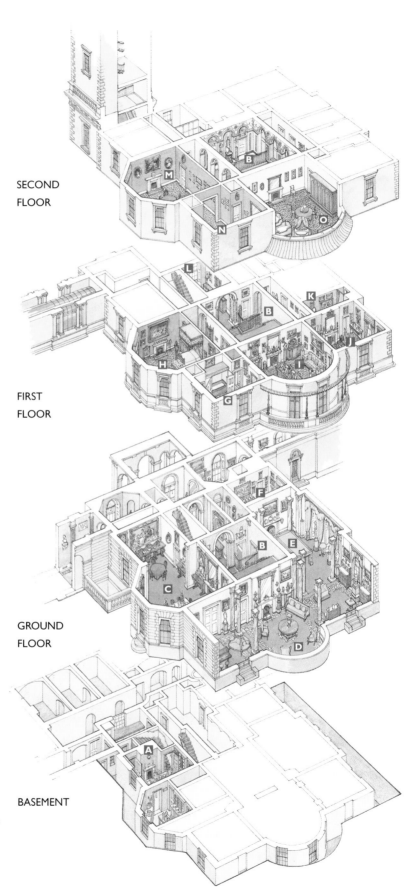

SECOND FLOOR

FIRST FLOOR

GROUND FLOOR

BASEMENT

The Pavilion

A Table-deckers' rooms
B Grand staircase
C Dining room
D Drawing room
E Billiard room
F Horn room
G Queen Victoria's dressing room
H Queen Victoria's bedroom
I Queen Victoria's sitting room
J Prince Albert's dressing room
K Prince Albert's bathroom
L Pages' alcove
M Nursery sitting room
N Governess's bedroom
O Nursery bedroom

TABLE-DECKERS' ROOMS

Steep servants' stairs lead down to the Pavilion basement and the table-deckers' rooms, which are immediately beneath the dining room. The function of table-decker was unique to the royal household, and was within the department of the lord steward, who oversaw all the kitchen staff.

Table-deckers were responsible for laying the dining tables for lunch and dinner and arranging displays of flowers from the kitchen garden. They also made the final preparations to the food. This came from the kitchen court, situated about 100m away to prevent cooking smells reaching the dining room. The table-deckers needed a hot closet in its own small room to keep the food warm. Their rooms also contain ample cupboards for china and lead-lined sinks in the inner room for washing glasses. The room was used only as a store after the queen's death, so the Victorian painted decoration has largely survived, including the blue-painted walls inside the glazed cupboards – blue was believed to discourage flies.

4 DINING ROOM

The dining, drawing and billiard rooms are the main reception rooms in the Pavilion. They are all richly decorated and each has an elaborate ceiling painted in 1857 to designs by Gruner and restored by English Heritage. Carpeted stairs lead from the table-deckers' rooms to the dining room: food and plates were brought up directly and laid out on the large mahogany sideboard. This, and the four side tables, have lion monopodia legs and were designed by Henry Whitaker in about 1847.

In the 1850s dinner was served promptly at 8pm. Towards the end of the century it shifted to 8.45pm, but it was often 9.15pm before the queen arrived and the company could sit down to eat. One of the dining tables shows the laying for dinner in progress, with the set square and ruler used by the table-deckers to ensure each setting was perfect. Osborne has no breakfast room, so breakfast was sometimes taken here when it was too cold for the queen to eat outside.

Family portraits always hung in this room. The largest, above the sideboard, is a Victorian copy of the family by Franz Xaver Winterhalter (1805–73) hung here on Victoria's birthday in 1849. To its left is a Victorian copy of Winterhalter's portrait of the Duchess of Kent, Victoria's mother.

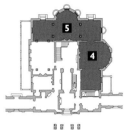

Left: The drawing room in the 1870s. It was initially lit by candles in the three cut-glass chandeliers made by Osler's of Birmingham
Below: One of the pair of pedestal chandeliers by Osler's, whose design Prince Albert supervised and which were displayed at the Great Exhibition of 1851

Facing page top:
Table-deckers' scullery below the dining room
Facing page bottom:
The dining room

The marriage of Princess Alice to Prince Louis of Hesse took place here in 1862. Overshadowed by the continued mourning for the Prince Consort, who had died the previous December, it was described by the queen as 'more like a funeral'. It was also in this room that the queen's body lay in state in 1901 before being taken to Windsor.

⑤ DRAWING ROOM

Victoria described the drawing room in 1846 as 'extremely handsome, with its yellow damask satin curtains and furniture to match'. The room was restored in 2003 to reflect its appearance in the 1890s, with repainted walls, curtains and upholstery based on archive samples, and a copy of the intricately patterned Aubusson carpet, which was made to fit the marbled columns in the room.

Full-length mirrors in heavy shutters reflected the brilliant candlelight from the three cut-glass chandeliers by Osler's of Birmingham (the current chandeliers are replicas). The pair of cut-glass pedestal chandeliers near the bay window are original and were also made by Osler's. All the chandeliers were wired for electricity in 1893.

The room was furnished more sparsely and formally until the 1870s. That it appeared formal even at the time is evident from a remark made in 1858 by Mary Bulteel, lady-in-waiting to Victoria, which also gives an insight into Albert's enthusiasm for scientific theories: 'I have routed the pianoforte out from the wall, to sit with one's face towards the people, instead of one's back; put the sofa crooked, with the round table near it, instead of stiffly in the middle of the room; the armchair crookedly and comfortably near the fire. If P.A. [Prince Albert] says anything about the pianoforte I shall stop his mouth with a little bit of scientific theory about the properties stone walls have of absorbing sound.'

This room contains some idealized statues of Victoria's children carved by Mary Thornycroft from 1845 to 1860, with a mixture of family portraits and landscapes.

Visiting foreign royalty were received in the drawing room and the queen generally retired here after dinner to play cards or to sing and play at the Erard piano with members of the household. Both the piano and six cabinets surmounting the bookcases are decorated with porcelain plaques painted by Carl Schmidt showing miniature copies of Italian Old Master paintings. Celebrated musicians also gave recitals here, including the soprano Jenny Lind (1820–87), known as the 'Swedish nightingale', who appeared

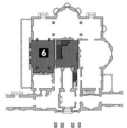

Ground floor

Left: The billiard room. George Magnus made both the billiard table and the cue stand by the end wall. His works were near Cubitt's yard in Pimlico, London, and the table was probably transported to Osborne on one of Cubitt's barges
Below: Cardinal Wolsey at the Gate of Leicester Abbey, *commissioned for the billiard room in 1847 by Prince Albert from Charles West Cope (1811–90)*

Facing page: The drawing room, restored in 2003 to reflect its appearance in the 1890s, with replica soft-furnishings, including the Aubusson carpet, and electrified chandeliers

at Osborne in 1847 (three months after her debut in London) with Luigi Lablache, the celebrated bass singer, from whom the queen had singing lessons.

6 BILLIARD ROOM

The right-angled plan of the billiard room, with its columned screen and drawn curtains, allowed the room to remain out of view from the adjacent drawing room so that the men could play billiards after dinner and sit on the raised bench while the queen remained in the next room. Technically, the men were still within the queen's presence, and protocol required them to stand unless given permission to sit. Above the bench is *Cardinal Wolsey at the Gate of Leicester Abbey*, by Charles West Cope (1811–90).

The slate billiard table was manufactured by Magnus. The legs were enamelled to represent marble and the frieze panels were designed by Albert, as was the elaborate light fitting. It was converted to electricity in 1893 (the original bank of brass light switches for this room with wiring hidden behind timber 'capping and casing' survives to the right of the door). The queen learnt to play billiards at Osborne and her journal records games with the women of the household after lunch.

A door leads to the principal stairwell, the walls of which were painted by the 'decorative artist' Anthony Muller in 1861 (who also worked at Buckingham Palace). William Theed's posthumous bust of the Prince Consort sits on a marble base, which houses a ventilator – part of Cubitt's heating system, which was controlled by a coal-fired boiler in the basement. The steep servants' back stairs have a simple handrail and iron balusters, and gave access to all the upper floors.

Above: One of the many babies' limbs, which the queen had sculpted in marble
Right: Pen drawing by Albert of the Princess Royal and the Prince of Wales, 1843
Below: The nursery bedroom, recreated as it was in a photograph of 1873

NURSERY

The nursery suite gives an insight into Queen Victoria and Prince Albert's relations with their young family. It was sited immediately above the couple's private apartments to allow them easy access to the children, who normally remained there until the age of six.

The first and second rooms originally formed the sitting room and bedroom of Lady Lyttelton, the superintendent of the royal children until 1851. Her role in overseeing the wellbeing of the children was wide-ranging; she described some of her duties in 1849: 'Accounts, tradesmen's letters, maids' quarrels, bad fitting of frocks, desirableness of rhubarb and magnesia, and, by way of intellectual pursuits, false French genders and elements of the multiplication table'.

Folding doors originally divided the two rooms, but these were removed during alterations in 1903 to accommodate the house governor of

the convalescent home. The wallpaper has not survived, so English Heritage repainted both rooms to match the aqua-green 'builder's finish' found elsewhere in the house.

7 Nursery Sitting Room

The first room became the schoolroom for the children of Prince and Princess Henry of Battenberg in the 1890s. It has been restored as the nursery sitting room, and contains framed photographs that show how the present royal families of Europe, both reigning and exiled, are descended from Queen Victoria. The queen and Prince Albert had nine children and made ambitious plans for their marriages. They looked to the European royal families for suitable partners to create a network of diplomatic and royal connections that they hoped would help secure peace and stability in Europe.

With the Prussian–Danish conflict of 1863, however, and the Prussian–Austrian war of 1866 the queen realized that the policy of cementing foreign alliances by marriage was not capable of halting European wars. This fact was tragically underlined when the First World War broke out in 1914 between Germany, led by her grandson, Kaiser Wilhelm II, and Britain. Nevertheless it is through the marriages of the children of Victoria and Albert that the present monarchs of Britain, Spain, Norway, Denmark and Sweden trace their ancestry to Queen Victoria.

8 Nursery Bedroom

The third room, the nursery bedroom, was often visited by the couple. It has been restored to match its appearance in a photograph taken in about 1873 by Jabez Hughes, a commercial photographer from Ryde, Isle of Wight, who recorded many of the buildings and interiors on the Osborne estate for Queen Victoria. By this date it was used on visits by the queen's grandchildren. None of the original decoration survived and the wallpaper, carpet and curtains are all modern. The swing cot with its mahogany frame was made for Vicky, the Princess Royal, in 1840. The cots, two of which are reproductions, have hinged cane-work sides and upholstered pads to protect the children. The screen shielded them from draughts, and a nurse slept in the bed. Several high chairs were used, similar to the one on display, which has an adjustable foot rail.

Many of the paintings, most of which originally hung here, had special associations for the queen and her family. Above the cots hangs a portrait of Albert, who painted the owl above the washstand

Second floor

when he was 17. Below it is a copy of a sketch by Victoria of Eos, Albert's favourite greyhound.

'All round the room are literally stacks of toys,' a member of the household commented in the 1890s. Now almost all that remain are Princess Louise's wicker trug and Princess Helena's exercise clubs. The doll's house is a copy of a German original of the mid 19th century in the photograph.

The remaining rooms on this floor were used as maids' bedrooms and the nursery kitchen.

Above: A 19th-century German musical box. The figures move to music from Tannhäuser, by Richard Wagner (1813–83)
Below: Painting in the nursery bedroom by J Lucas of Prince Albert, Princess Victoria and Eos, his favourite greyhound, from Coburg (1843)

Right: The allegorical fresco Neptune Resigning the Empire of the Seas to Britannia *demonstrated Britain's supremacy as a world power. Neptune, in a shell chariot drawn by three seahorses, hands his crown via Mercury (messenger to the gods) to Britannia, who already holds Neptune's trident. Beside her is the lion of England. The figures behind her represent industry, trade and navigation*

Below: The pages' alcove, as redecorated to its original scheme in 2005. It contains modern copies of the bells that summoned the pages

9 STAIRCASE

The grand staircase was modelled on that at Claremont House, Surrey, belonging to Victoria's uncle Leopold (1790–1865), who became King of the Belgians in 1831. The walls were painted by Anthony Muller. At the head of the stairs is a life-size statue of Prince Albert in classical armour, commissioned by him from the German sculptor Emil Wolf (1802–79) as a birthday present to the queen in 1842. It was not completed until 1844. Albert considered its 'bare legs & feet, looked too undressed to place in a room' so in 1849 a suitably shod copy was made for Buckingham Palace.

Profiles in marble of Frederick and Victoria (the queen's eldest daughter), the Crown Prince and Princess of Prussia, are inserted into the over-doors to left and right. The left-hand door originally led to the nursery kitchen; that to the right is a plaster dummy for the sake of symmetry.

Also at the head of the stairs is the large fresco *Neptune Resigning the Empire of the Seas to Britannia* by William Dyce (1806–64), who came to Osborne in 1847 to paint it. Lady Lyttelton, whose rooms were next to it, probably saw more of him than most. She was not impressed, calling him, 'one of the least agreeable, and most dry and half-sneering mannered men I have ever met'.

10 PAGES' ALCOVE

The pages' alcove is off the first-floor landing. A page of the back stairs was in attendance at the door of the queen's apartment from 8am until she retired at night. Some of Prince Albert's early Renaissance pictures were hung here, including three by Cranach the Elder (1472–1553).

The porcelain medallions bearing various Christian and classical designs are by the Danish sculptor Albert Bertel Thorvaldsen (1770–1844). The Royal Danish Porcelain Manufactory produced them in the 1840s and they are another example of the high-quality but commercially available pieces the prince chose.

The first floor was symmetrically planned about the east–west axis of the Pavilion to accommodate the private apartments of Victoria and Albert.

The room to the left was intended to be the prince's bedroom (not open to the public). It was little, if ever, used by him, however, and by the 1870s had become a schoolroom. Beyond are Albert's bathroom and his dressing and writing room. In the centre is the sitting room used by both Albert and Victoria, while the rooms on the right comprised the queen's domain: her dressing room and bedroom.

▥ PRINCE ALBERT'S BATHROOM

The bathroom contains a plumbed-in bath, lavatory and shower – unusual in the mid 19th century. A large fresco of 1830 by A von Gegenbauer depicts Hercules laying aside his power and becoming a slave to Omphale, Queen of Lydia, possibly suggesting Albert's attitude to Victoria. On the walls are some paintings by the couple and photographs of tableaux enacted by the children.

▦ PRINCE ALBERT'S DRESSING AND WRITING ROOM

The dual function of this room is indicated by its contents: a dwarf wardrobe, washstand, and writing table. In the 19th century the walls were hung with Albert's most precious early Renaissance pictures, almost exclusively religious. They included works by Mantegna, Bellini and Fra Angelico, some of which are now in the National Gallery in London. Above the chimney-glass is a double portrait of Albert and his brother Ernest by Louise von Meyern-Hohenburg of 1841. Victoria bought it two years after her marriage.

Albert's bathroom and dressing room were kept by the widowed queen as far as possible as they had been during his life. She frequently used his dressing room for private, informal audiences. Randall Davidson, her chaplain from 1883 to 1891, was received by her many times in the prince's dressing room. He observed, 'Hot water was actually brought to his dressing room at dressing-time 40 years after his death … I have again and again had talks to her there before dinner with the hot water actually steaming.' Davidson believed the practice continued because at first the queen ordered that nothing was to be changed until she gave further instructions. The servants could not bring themselves to challenge those instructions, and as the years passed there was nothing to lead her to give contrary orders.

Second floor

First floor

Above: *Painting by Victoria entitled* Closing Scene from 'Der Hahnenschlag'. *In 1852, the children enacted this German play by A F F von Kotzbue at Windsor Castle. In the foreground are Princesses Louise and Helena in costume*
Left: *Prince Albert's dressing and writing room, where he would read or write in his 'golden morning hour' before the queen was up*

⑬ QUEEN VICTORIA'S SITTING ROOM

This room, at the centre of the first floor of the Pavilion, has commanding views from the bow window across the terraces and parkland to the Solent. During the day the couple worked on the dispatch-boxes here, which constantly arrived from London via the queen's messengers.

Victoria sat at the left-hand desk. The three mid 19th-century bell pulls were connected to an early electric battery powered by chemical action. They would have summoned Miss Skerrett (the queen's principal dresser and confidante), a page, and Rudolf Löhlein, a Coburger and a personal attendant to Albert, and later to the queen. The prince's desk to the right is identical, except that the drawers are shallower to allow for his longer legs. Albert worked here while submitting memoranda for the queen's inspection in his capacity as her private and personal secretary.

'When I am not particularly occupied,' wrote the queen in 1846, 'Vicky and Bertie alternately always take their supper in our room. Then little Helena is brought down for a quarter of an hour, followed by Affie, and then Alice.' The queen and prince could also withdraw to this room informally after dinner, either alone or with close friends. If alone, the couple might occupy themselves by pasting prints, woodcuts or sketches of places they had visited into albums, or by discussing one of Albert's projects, such as his photographic record of the complete works of Raphael. Victoria's journal includes references to watching the moonlight shining on the Solent from the balcony, and listening to the nightingales in the trees below. A contemporary recorded that Victoria's rooms always smelt of orange flower.

Behind the sofa is *The Good Samaritan* by Sir Charles Eastlake (1793–1865), who was keeper of the National Gallery from 1843 to 1847. After Albert's death Victoria accumulated the memorabilia which fill the room and include many portraits, photographs and busts of her family, including the plaster statuette by Boehm of the queen spinning with a collie at her feet, made in 1869. The actual spinning wheel nearby was made on the Athole (Atholl) estate in Scotland by John McGlashan aged 70 and was given to the queen by the dowager Duchess of Atholle in 1866.

First floor

Facing page: Queen Victoria's sitting room with her desk and Prince Albert's side by side beneath a large ormolu (gilt brass) lamp made to burn viscous colza, a vegetable oil, gravity-fed from the raised reservoir

Left: This remarkably sensual painting, Florinda, by F X Winterhalter, 1852, was bought that year by the queen for £1,000 for Albert's birthday. It was returned to Osborne in March 2011 and hangs again as it did originally opposite the desks of Victoria and Albert in the queen's sitting room

14 QUEEN VICTORIA'S DRESSING ROOM

This room contains a bath which, following contemporary propriety, looks like a wardrobe with full-length mirrors when not in use. Next to it is a shower, equally well disguised. In the narrow passage to the left is the queen's lavatory. Access to it from her bedroom was cleverly disguised to look like part of a large mahogany wardrobe.

15 QUEEN VICTORIA'S BEDROOM

The pattern of the printed cotton of the bed hangings, sofa and curtains incorporates profiles of the couple, and was designed for the royal yacht *Victoria and Albert* in the 1850s. Its use here is modern. Above the fireplace is *The Entombment* by Gustav Jäger (1808–71), commissioned by Albert in 1845. His fascination with gadgets is

Above: Portrait of Annie Macdonald, one of a pair by Queen Victoria of the children of a Balmoral gillie, painted in 1852, the year Albert acquired the Balmoral estate

Right: Queen Victoria's dressing table, with the fine Minton porcelain dressing table set commissioned by Prince Albert as a Christmas present in 1853

demonstrated by the brass device that allowed the door to be bolted and unbolted from the bed. A pocket for his watch is fixed to the headboard next to a posthumous portrait of him which the widowed queen displayed in each residence.

On 22 January 1901 Queen Victoria died in this room on a small couch bed, surrounded by her children. For the next 50 years, the bedroom was set up as a family shrine, with a bronze memorial plaque on the headboard, the blinds pulled down, and an 'altar' constructed from a plans chest draped with a cloth and supporting a cross and candlesticks. In 1955 these most intimate apartments were opened to the public by permission of Queen Elizabeth II.

Outside the bedroom is an iron gate. Edward VII erected this, and the gate in the opposite corridor, after Queen Victoria's death to prevent access to these rooms which, as a general rule, were opened only to members of the royal family.

First floor

Left: Queen Victoria's bedroom, showing the bronze plaque in her memory, designed by Queen Alexandra and Alfred Young Nutt, clerk of works at Windsor Castle

Below: A hand-coloured photograph of the bedroom from the 1850s. Some photographs were coloured by the queen and others by professional artists

Birthdays at Osborne

After dressing in a new summer frock, the queen was greeted at the foot of the stairs by all her children carrying nosegays

From 1848 until Albert's death, Victoria was nearly always at Osborne for her birthday on 24 May. The day started at 7am with a band playing below her bedroom window – often the tune was one of Albert's hymns. After dressing in a new summer frock and giving Albert one or two presents, the queen was greeted at the foot of the stairs by her children carrying nosegays. As in her childhood, a birthday table was set out in a room decorated with flowers. In 1848 and 1849 the horn room was used, but by the 1850s a spare bedroom in the main wing was established as the 'present room'. Breakfast followed in the dining room, sometimes with the band still playing on the terrace. The day often concluded after dinner with dancing in the council room.

Albert, too, was almost invariably at Osborne for his birthday on 26 August. In 1851 the children sang outside his dressing room before taking him to the present room. There followed a French play acted by the five eldest children and as a treat the four eldest sat with their parents at the dinner table that evening for the first time. Throughout the 19th century a 'rustic fête' was held for the estate workers in honour of Albert's birthday, including a band, games such as sack races, climbing a greasy pole for a leg of mutton, and bobbing for oranges, and dinner in a marquee.

Children's birthdays started in the schoolroom, from where their parents escorted them to the dining room to find their presents arranged on a table. In 1848 the queen records that Princess Alice was given 'a live little lamb all decked out with ribbons … We had it tamed by Toward's [the estate steward's] daughter. It is a sweet gentle little thing.' The animal painter Thomas Sidney Cooper (1803–1902) painted Milly the lamb at Barton Farm and gave the painting to the princess.

Right: Queen Victoria's birthday table at Osborne, 24 May 1848, painted by Joseph Nash the Elder (1809–78). The two glass pedestal chandeliers given by Albert are displayed in the drawing room

🔟 HORN ROOM

The door to the horn room on the right of the corridor has been half-glazed. It is kept closed to protect the 19th-century carpet and wallpaper. This room was the setting for some of Queen Victoria's birthday tables (see opposite page). Prince Albert bought the remarkable collection of antler furniture (attributed to F Bohler of Frankfurt) in 1845 – even the circular table is inlaid with sections of deer horn. In 1847 the royal couple stayed at Ardverikie, in Inverness, before visiting Balmoral for the first time. They brought back stags' horns which they arranged in the horn room at Osborne that September.

In 1989 Landseer's moving portrait of Queen Victoria was returned to this room, where it was first hung in 1867. Alternately titled *Osborne 1865* and *Sorrow*, it depicts the widowed queen in the broad walk at Osborne seated on her pony Flora, reading a despatch. John Brown, her Highland servant, is clad in the mourning kilt the queen devised for him. Behind, on a bench, sit Princesses Louise and Helena in lilac half-mourning dresses. The painting was exhibited at the Royal Academy in 1867, and further fuelled unfounded speculation about the queen's relationship with Brown.

In the corridor on the left are two pictures of the Georgian Osborne House, one of which was ingeniously drawn in 1844 using multi-coloured Alum Bay sand – an art form popular on the island in the 19th century.

QUEEN VICTORIA'S LIFT

This passenger lift was installed by Otis in 1893 to allow the increasingly infirm queen easier access to her first-floor apartments. She was wheeled in her 'rolling chair' into the lift which was hand-operated by an attendant in the basement. Outside the lift, in the corner, is a jib-door behind which a footman clad in livery of scarlet coat and white stockings could observe the carriage ring for signs of the queen's carriage approaching.

This corridor area was formerly a guest bedroom before it was converted into part of the corridor linking the newly built Durbar wing of 1890–91. The dado is covered with Lincrusta, an embossed wall-covering popular at the time.

A pair of half-glazed doors pierce the original external wall of the Pavilion and lead into the Durbar Corridor, which also has a Lincrusta dado.

Ground floor

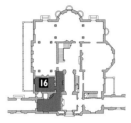

Left: Horn furniture similar to this was displayed in the Great Exhibition of 1851, and enjoyed increased popularity after that date

Below: The horn room was sometimes used as a visitors' sitting room

Queen Victoria and India

The queen wrote to her daughter-in-law, 'I have such a great longing to go to India … I have been thinking of it very much of late'

Queen Victoria was created Empress of India by Disraeli in 1876. In 1887 her son Prince Arthur, Duke of Connaught, was serving in India as commander-in-chief of the Bombay Army. The queen wrote to her daughter-in-law, 'I have such a great longing to go to India … You may think me crazy for saying this – but I can assure you I have been thinking of it – very much of late.' The visit never took place, but in June 1887 the queen took on two Indian servants, the first of many, at Osborne. An extension to the male servants' barracks was built to house them, and in the 1890s the surveyor of works regularly recorded his men preparing curry stones (for grinding spices) for them to use.

The Indian servants wore turbans and a livery of scarlet and gold in winter and white in summer. It was embroidered with the monogram VRI (*Victoria Regina et Imperatrix* – Victoria Queen and Empress). One of these, Abdul Karim, was an ambitious 24-year-old Muslim who in 1889 was promoted to the post of munshi (secretary or tutor), teaching the queen Hindi. Jealousies arose within the household, however, and, while Karim claimed his father was a surgeon-general in India, his status was called into question. Victoria asked Frederick Ponsonby, who was appointed equerry while serving in India, to make enquiries. On his return Ponsonby told the queen, truthfully but tactlessly, that Karim's father was druggist to the gaol in Agra. The queen was deeply offended and refused to invite Ponsonby to lunch for a year.

Above right: Portrait of Abdul Karim, Queen Victoria's Indian secretary, by Rudolf Swoboda, 1888, in the white- and gold-striped turban that the queen decreed should be worn at dinner time

Right: Fine examples of Indian craftsmanship presented to the queen by her Indian subjects, revealing the same intricacy of surface detail found on a larger scale in the Durbar Room

A *Lacquerwork address case from Hyderabad, Sind, 1887*

B *Velvet inner cover of address case (above)*

C *Silver elephant address casket from the Rao of Kutch, 1897*

D *Ivory workbox from the Raja of Bobbili, 1893*

A

B

C

D

Durbar Wing

⑰ DURBAR CORRIDOR

The new wing was constructed in 1890–91 to house Prince and Princess Henry of Battenberg and their family on the first floor. Princess Henry (Beatrice) was Victoria's youngest daughter. The queen was so dependent on her in later years that when Beatrice unofficially announced her engagement in 1883, the queen did not speak to her for six months. She was given permission to marry in 1885, on the understanding that she continued to live with the queen.

In the Durbar Corridor and Durbar Room, the queen could create a tangible reminder of the land that she would never visit. The paintings in the Durbar Corridor reflect the queen's interest in her Indian empire and its people. The most imposing portrait is that of the maharaja Duleep Singh, commissioned by the queen from Winterhalter in 1854. Nearby on the left-hand wall are three small paintings on porcelain of the maharaja, his wife the maharanee Bamba, and their son Victor Albert, named in honour of the royal couple.

The section of the corridor running the length of the Durbar wing contains a unique and extensive collection of Indian portraits by the Austrian portraitist Rudolf Swoboda (1859–1914). In 1886 London hosted the Colonial and Indian Exhibition, which included a living display of over 30 Indian craftsmen. Swoboda had recently been introduced to the queen and she commissioned him to paint some of those craftsmen. Enthused by his paintings, she then commissioned him to go to India to sketch 'various types of different nationalities'. He travelled in India from 1886 to

1888 and produced 43 closely observed studies from life. The portraits were hung as a group in the Durbar Corridor on its completion in 1894, together with his portraits of some of the queen's Indian servants, including Abdul Karim, the munshi, and the designer Bhai Ram Singh. The queen considered his portraits 'beautiful things' and they form an important record of a wide cross-section of Indian society, ages and occupations.

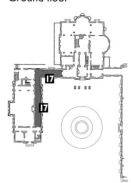

Ground floor

Above left: Duleep Singh, by F X Winterhalter, 1854, commissioned the year the 15-year-old maharaja stayed at Osborne

Below: A selection of the framed Indian portraits by Rudolf Swoboda, 1886–8, in the Durbar Corridor

⬛ DURBAR ROOM

'Durbar' is derived from an Indian word meaning both a state reception and the hall in which it is held, so the room is aptly named both for its function and its Indian style of architecture, which was briefly popular towards the end of the 19th century. While serving in India, Prince Arthur, the Duke of Connaught, met Lockwood Kipling (father of Rudyard) who was director of the Mayo School of Art at Lahore in the Punjab. In 1884 the billiard room at Connaught's home, Bagshot Park, Surrey, was decorated in Indian style as a gift from the

Indian princes. The carving was done in Lahore by Bhai Ram Singh under the supervision of Kipling, and Connaught introduced their work to the queen. In August 1890 Kipling was asked to submit an Indian design for the new room at Osborne. The queen and Princess Louise made suggestions to improve the design and in January 1891 Kipling arrived at Osborne with Ram Singh.

Design and Decoration

J R Mann's plan of the Durbar Room suggests a medieval great hall, with a screens passage and minstrels' gallery at the 'low' end and the servery beyond. The decoration is inspired by the architectural traditions of north India – a fusion, sometimes described as Indo-Saracenic, of Islamic forms and detail from Hindu and Jain temples, which looks back to the Mogul architecture of the 16th and 17th centuries. This flamboyant version includes an unusual variety of detail, effectively creating a unique room for English court protocol in the Indian style.

Ram Singh designed and carved the wooden moulds used by the plasterers, Jacksons of London. The surfaces are enriched with plaster and *carton pierre* – a type of papier mâché common in the late 19th century – the white walls being further enlivened by teak framing. The dado panels ornamented with vases of flowers resemble the types of *pietra dura* design (inlay using hard stones) found on the walls of Mogul monuments such as the Taj Mahal. The cornice and overmantel are ornamented with multiple niches, a form found in Indian Islamic architecture from the 12th century onwards. The wall above the screen is set with chattris, a type of domed canopy favoured in Mogul design. The decoration includes the Indian symbols of Ganesh – the elephant god of good fortune – over the door near the gallery.

Princess Louise suggested a peacock over the chimneypiece in November 1890. Jacksons had 26 craftsmen working on the chimneypiece and overmantel, and more than 500 hours were spent on the peacock alone, equivalent to one man working solidly for ten weeks. The deeply coffered ceiling is derived from the ceiling ornament found in medieval temple structures such as the Jain temples at Mount Abu, Rajasthan.

Ram Singh also designed the brass door handles in the form of a bird and the brass lamp

Above: The peacock chimneypiece. The peacock is a common Indian motif
Right: Bhai Ram Singh from the Lahore School of Art, India, at work in the Durbar Room in 1891. He designed and carved the wooden moulds for the plasterwork. The photograph shows the exposed timber battens supporting plasterwork on the end wall

Ground floor

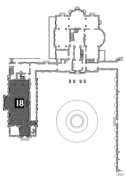

Left: The Durbar Room, Christmas 1896, with a tree and tables of presents
Below: One of the original set of 36 dining chairs designed for the room by Bhai Ram Singh. The furniture was disposed of in 1916, but English Heritage bought nine chairs with the help of the National Art Collections Fund, the Heritage Lottery Fund, the Island Friends of Royal Osborne and the Duleep Singh Trust. Replicas have been made for visitors to use

stands. In February 1893, the queen wrote, 'We dined in the Durbar Room which was lit by electric light & looked beautiful.' She was won over to electricity and by September 1894 most of the building was lit with Edison & Swan lamps.

Display

The room contains a display of gifts from the sub-continent commemorating Victoria's golden and diamond jubilees of 1887 and 1897. Address caskets – decorative boxes containing loyal greetings to the queen – form most of the collection. They were sent from every part of the Indian empire and give a rare snapshot of Indian craftsmanship at the end of the 19th century. One of the most beautiful is a replica of the great gun of Bijapur, a cannon cast in Agra in 1549. Some are

very rare, such as those decorated with sadeli work (geometrical inlay of tiny pieces of ivory, metal and coloured woods). The exquisite model of a palace in Jaipur is made from plaster, painted and gilded. Even the interiors are recreated in colourful detail.

To mark the centenary of the queen's death in 2001, the collection was redisplayed in new cases, and the original carpet from Agra, the curtains, and the lighting (with replica bulbs) copied to recreate the appearance of the room in about 1900.

The lobby at the far end of the Durbar Room was originally a private entrance hall serving the Battenbergs' apartments. At the other end, the right-hand door beneath the minstrels' gallery leads to the former Durbar servery, which has a visitors' exit and ramp on to the terrace.

Tour of the Gardens

TERRACES

Gruner helped to design and lay out the Italianate terraces at the head of the valley with Prince Albert and Cubitt. Massive earth-moving was needed and the valley was remodelled to create the sweeping fall to the coast. Some of the terrace retaining walls are up to 25ft (7.6m) deep.

Pavilion Terrace

Gruner took items from Austin & Seeley's 1844 catalogue and arranged them to create a huge vase comprising four sphinxes with added wings supporting a fluted bowl. He also bought the surrounding statues of the Four Seasons supplied by Miroy Frères of Paris, and copies of Florentine and Roman originals from the catalogue of Geiss of Berlin, to enhance Osborne's Italianate qualities. In the salt-laden air the applied bronze corroded to reveal the zinc beneath, which in turn became pitted by the salts. The statues have now been recoated with a reversible acrylic compound to imitate the original patinated bronze.

The projecting square alcove to the left of the clock tower was used by Queen Victoria for breakfast, and for reading and writing.

The parterres on the terrace were initially framed by walkways of coloured imitation lava from Orsi & Armani of London. There was a rich variety of bedding plants: the queen writes in her journal of geraniums, heliotropes and the summer evening air scented with orange blossom, roses and jasmine. Excavations in 1994 uncovered the chalk footings to the elaborate beds which follow those on a mid 19th-century plan in the National Archives; these have been recreated. Historic bedding has been reinstated, using, where possible, plants introduced to Britain before the queen's death.

Lower Terrace

The lower terrace contains a triple-arched alcove flanked by steps. The shell alcove nearby has a canal-coal bench with dolphin supports and is decorated with shells from the beach. Victoria records a delightful observation in August 1852 of workmen fixing shells to the roof while a 'charming magpie' was taking all the shells. In the middle of the lower terrace is the Andromeda fountain by John Bell, surrounded by eight marine monsters by William Theed, cast in 1858–60. Other statues are copies of classical originals, including the hunter Meleager with his spear and hound.

Austin & Seeley's cement copies of the Medici lions in Florence, supplied in 1851, flank the lowest flight of steps beyond the fountain. The lions face

Above: The statue of Andromeda by John Bell, at the centre of the fountain on the lower terrace. Bell has depicted the mythological Andromeda in chains awaiting rescue by Perseus, her future husband
Right: View from the upper terrace of the Andromeda fountain and broad walk leading down the valley to the Solent

the lowest fountain of a bronze boy with a swan, from Geiss of Berlin. It sits at the head of the broad walk which has planters, reinstated in 2005, of clipped Portuguese laurel (*Prunus lusitanica*), as shown in Landseer's painting *Sorrow* (see page 46).

Upper Terrace

The horseshoe steps at the far end of the upper terrace lead down to a further lower terrace opposite the former orangery and Victoria Hall (both now part of the terrace restaurant). The orangery doors are white, unlike the rest of the external doors and windows of the main house which are red in imitation of mahogany. The cast heads in the keystones have all been adapted by Cubitt so that each is different; one on the right bears a strong resemblance to Prince Albert.

The adjoining Victoria Hall was originally a blind wall to screen the stable block and other service buildings. In the 1880s the arches were opened and a private chapel built behind so that the increasingly infirm queen could avoid services at Whippingham. It is now the terrace restaurant, where the stained glass and inscription above the chimneypiece indicate its original function.

Against the outside wall is the royal myrtle (*Myrtus communis*) grown from a sprig from the nosegay presented to the queen by the dowager Duchess of Saxe Gotha and Attenburg (Prince Albert's grandmother) when Victoria left Gotha on

3 September 1845. It has since been used in royal wedding bouquets as a symbol of the innocence of the bride, a German tradition.

Other significant plants here include the chusan palm (*Trachycarpus fortunei*), planted by the queen on her birthday in 1851, one of the first to be planted outside in this country. It was felled due to old age and Elizabeth II planted another in May 2004. The walls of the lower terrace are clothed with *Magnolia grandiflora* planted by Prince Albert.

On the low wall nearby are two artificial stone greyhounds flanking the path. The sloping walk beyond this wall leads up to the Swiss Cottage road. It contains a granite memorial bench on the yew walk, south of the orangery, where John Brown apparently used to read his letters from home. It is carved with a relief of Brown and an inscription suggested by Tennyson: 'A truer, nobler trustier heart, more loving and more loyal, never beat within a human breast.' The queen chose the quotation from a play by Byron, *The Two Foscari*, where – curiously – it is said by a wife in defence of her maligned husband.

Above: The Pavilion terrace in spring, with Gruner's sphinx vase at its centre, and the 1845 bronze statue of Eos, Prince Albert's favourite greyhound, by John Francis
Below: Ludwig Gruner's drawing for the sphinx vase on the Pavilion terrace, 1849. Gruner also designed other ornaments for the terraces and acted as the prince's agent in buying some of the cement and bronze-coated zinc statuary

WALLED GARDEN AND PLEASURE GROUNDS

The walled kitchen garden and adjoining pleasure grounds in front of the house remain as elements from the late 18th-century landscape. In 1843 the garden was described as 'fully cropped and stocked with choice standard and other trees', but towards the end of Victoria's reign the emphasis was on growing flowers for the house. The original cross-path layout has been restored and a garden added in 2000 to the design of Rupert Goldby. It incorporates trained Victorian fruit trees such as Lane's Prince Albert apples, Victoria plums and Brunswick figs, while further period fruit and roses overhang the new iron arches framing the paths. A cold-frame in the north-east corner is full in winter and spring with Victoria's favourite Parma violets.

The two Gothic lean-to glasshouses were erected in 1854 by Thomas Clark & Co of Birmingham. They copy the formerly extensive range of glasshouses built for Prince Albert at Frogmore, Windsor, in the 1840s.

Near the walled garden is a small timber octagonal summer house built by Cubitt in 1848. The children occasionally had their supper here. Cubitt heightened the front wall in 1848, disguised the brick buttresses to look like stone pilasters and in the centre placed the Portland stone entrance porch salvaged from old Osborne House.

Albert improved the pleasure grounds, where the family would stroll, by planting magnolias, rhododendrons and azaleas around the summer house. The walk along Swiss Cottage road follows the contours of the valley and provides an excellent view of Osborne and its terraces, as well as passing close to the ice house. The formal landscape near the house is in marked contrast to the parkland through which the visitor now passes.

Trees

By 1861 the estate had 400 acres of woodland, mainly around the park. The woodland was commercially managed, providing products such as hurdles and rods for fencing. Walks and rides were cut and ornamented for use by the royal family. The historic rides and views through the woods have been restored and are regularly maintained.

Throughout the park and pleasure grounds, an important visit, anniversary, birth or death might be commemorated by planting a memorial tree, of which at least 270 existed across the estate. Many were new introductions to Britain. Albert's planting scheme was partly dictated by his respect for the late 18th-century landscape of old Osborne House. Other influences included his liking for the poplars at the Rosenau and for the Italian fashion of lining drives and walks with evergreens such as myrtle and laurel. Barton Drive is planted with holm oak (*Quercus ilex*), which gives a Mediterranean feel to the curved avenue. The Sovereign's Drive is a double avenue of cedar of Lebanon and *Quercus 'Lucombeana'* (outer) and holm oak (inner).

Albert was intensely practical, and used the Pavilion's flag tower as a vantage point from which to direct gardeners in the positioning of flags to represent trees in the park. He strengthened the shelter belt of broad-leafed woodland in the outer park along the coast where native trees – oak, elm and beech – predominated. He left a clear view of the Solent either side of the valley to frame the house when seen from the sea, which was centred on the main wing, the site of old Osborne House.

Above: The classical entrance to the ice house. The supply of ice on the estate was unreliable and the queen preferred lake ice imported from the USA

Ice House

Ice was used to prepare food and to cool the dining room. The ice house was built by Cubitt in 1846 into the side of the hill, with a cavity wall for insulation. The floor is lined with bricks drilled with holes to drain melting ice. On 14 December 1846 the queen wrote, 'Went to see the ice house filled which is quite a curious performance. Hardest frost we have yet had. The men were breaking it above and throwing it down through an opening – we watched from below, ice falling like rain.' In the harsh winter of 1859, 60 cartloads of ice were packed into the ice house over two days. A classical entrance was added in 1853.

John Brown

John Brown (1826–83) was born in Crathienaird, Aberdeenshire, son of a tenant farmer. He came into the queen's service in 1848 as a gillie at Balmoral. By 1858 he had become her regular outside attendant, leading her pony on their Highland expeditions, helping cook potatoes on the moors, and lacing her tea with whisky.

The queen was so overwhelmed by Albert's death that she did not attend a public function until 1864. There was much concern for her health and in 1864 it was suggested that Brown be brought to Osborne to encourage her to ride her pony. He arrived in December and Victoria soon made the arrangement permanent, giving Brown the title 'the queen's Highland servant'. She wrote, 'I feel I have here always in the House a good, devoted Soul … whose only object & interest is my service, & God knows how much I want to be taken care of.'

But Brown's forthright manner made him enemies and he could be blunt to the point of rudeness: the lord chancellor dismissed him as a 'coarse animal'. Brown would address the queen as 'wumman', but she overlooked his faults, including his increasing dependence on whisky which, to use her euphemism, made him 'bashful'. Given the nature of the queen's relative seclusion in the 1870s it is easy to see how

'I feel I have here always in the House a good, devoted Soul … whose only object & interest is my service'

unfounded rumours spread of Brown's relationship to her, the mildest of which was their supposed marriage.

Victoria was inconsolable after Brown's death in March 1883: 'It is the loss not only of a servant but of a real friend.' Sir Henry Ponsonby, her private secretary, wrote a balanced view: 'He was the only person who could fight and make the Queen do what she did not wish. He did not always succeed, nor was his advice always the best. But I believe he was honest, and with all his want of education, his roughness, his prejudices, and other faults, he was undoubtedly a most excellent servant to her.'

Above: John Brown in his grey Osborne kilt, devised as a form of half-mourning by the queen in 1861. Victoria commissioned the watercolour by Kenneth MacLeay (1802–78) as part of a series called Highlanders of Scotland, published in two volumes in 1870. She gave a set to John Brown that Christmas

Plan of Swiss Cottage area

A Summer house

B Children's garden plots

C Swiss Cottage

D Swiss Cottage museum

E Wildflower garden and fountain

F Gazelle house

G Victoria Fort and Albert Barracks

Swiss Cottage

SWISS COTTAGE GARDEN

These grounds formed part of Albert's educational programme for his children and were given to them in 1850. Many aspects of his own education were recreated, including a children's garden, Swiss cottage, model fort and museum. The children had identical plots arranged into beds to grow flowers, fruits and vegetables that they sold to Albert at commercial rates as an exercise in market gardening. The gardens were left as used by the children until 1905, when given over to flowers. Now fruit and vegetables that would have been available in the 19th century are again grown here. They are largely maintained organically and often allowed to run to seed so that old varieties no longer available commercially can be propagated.

A thatched summer house west of the cottage held the children's scaled-down tools and barrows, each painted with its owner's initials (replicas are

Above: The frieze of the Swiss Cottage is carved with improving quotations in German, including, 'You will carry your load more easily if you add patience to the burden'

Right: Some of the children's plots in the Swiss Cottage garden

on display). Queen Victoria stated that Bertie and Affie (see page 44) helped lay the brick floor. The walls and roof were rebuilt in 1882. The Office of Works added metal gates in 1904 and in 2003 it was rethatched with straw and 'liggers' (hazel strips to fix thatch), imitating the 19th-century pattern.

Wildflower Garden and Gazelle House

Beyond the Swiss Cottage is a paddock that has been managed as a wildflower area for more than 100 years. It was given Coronation Meadow status in 2013 in a project led by the Prince of Wales to protect and celebrate meadows of great richness and mark the Queen's diamond jubilee. In 1907 the Office of Works added the fountain, with its basin and statue of lead, cast from models by Felix Joubert of the fashionable Chelsea decorators and cabinet-makers, and its base of Portland stone.

The historic orchard to the north has been reinstated, planted with a range of old varieties of

apple, pear, cherry, plum, gage, quince, medlar, mulberry and nut. Nearby is the timber gazelle house built in the 1860s and replaced in 1872. It is now a cake shop. It takes its name from a family of gazelles that lived here in the early 1860s as part of a small menagerie. In later years a colony of Angora rabbits was housed in hutches in the paddock, their wool used by Princess Beatrice, who spun and wove it into items for local bazaars.

SWISS COTTAGE

In 1853 the royal children laid the foundation stone of a timber cottage to the east of Osborne House. It sits on a rubble plinth and originally had a timber roof weighted down with rocks in the Alpine manner. The furnished cottage was given to the children on Queen Victoria's birthday in 1854.

Above: The Swiss Cottage with rocks on the roof. These imitate a real Alpine building, where they prevent the wind from lifting the roof. They were removed in 1932 and some can be seen built into the bank beside the visitor WCs

Left: The thatched summer house in the garden of the Swiss Cottage, housing replicas of the chidlren's painted barrows

Below: The meadow beyond the Swiss Cottage, which has been managed as a wildflower garden for more than 100 years. The fountain with its lead statue was added in 1907

First-floor plan

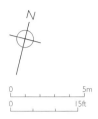

0   5m
0   15ft

Ground-floor plan

   1854

::::::::   1854 missing walls

HR = housekeeper's rooms

Above: *Floor plans of the Swiss Cottage*
Right: *The Swiss Cottage in 1855 by W L Leitch. The inspiration for a Swiss cottage may have come from Queen Victoria's half-sister, Princess Feodore of Hoehenlohe Langenberg, who wrote to the queen in 1851 that she had built a little Swiss cottage for her children in the garden of the Villa Friesenberg at Baden-Baden. An Alpine chalet dating from the 1830s with German quotations is also a feature of Shrubland, Suffolk, which Prince Albert visited in 1851*

The first-floor balcony and other details imitate a traditional Swiss farmhouse. It has a frieze carved in German with proverbs and quotations from the Psalms, doubtless intended by Albert to guide his children through life. The external logs were coated with burnt umber, a deep brown colour, but covered with black tar in the 20th century. They have now been repainted brown.

In 1867 it was claimed that the cottage was built 'in exact imitation of a Swiss chalet, and the furniture, ornaments, and decoration for it, were expressly imported from Switzerland', but the evidence suggests otherwise. It was designed in imperial measurements, with main dimensions of 25 × 50ft (6.6 × 15.2m). Metal fixings were applied instead of using the logs in a structural way. Analysis in 1990 suggested that the logs are *Pinus strobus*, a North American pine. The cottage may have been prefabricated in England and erected at Osborne by local carpenters supervised by the surveyor of works, John Blandford (d.1857). But the cast-iron casement windows may well have been imported, as the circular glazing pattern is rare in England. An 1856 plan and elevation of the cottage is signed 'G.S.', who is as yet unidentified.

Albert intended the cottage to be somewhere his children could learn the rudiments of cookery and housekeeping, and entertain their parents. As boys, he and his brother Ernest had created a natural history museum in Coburg. Albert set aside a room at the Swiss Cottage where his children could build a similar collection. Objects came from all over the world and the collection grew so that a separate museum was built nearby in 1862.

Housekeeper's Rooms, Larder, Scullery and Kitchen

Louise Warne, the cottage housekeeper, lived with her husband, Thomas, on the ground floor in four rooms (now three and housing an exhibition). Among her duties was the care of a chihuahua given in 1856 to the queen, who described it as 'a curious little dog brought from Mexico – something like a diminutive Italian greyhound'.

The room tiled on only three walls was the children's larder; the fourth wall was removed before 1941. Here butter was churned and fruit and vegetables stored. It leads through a reopened doorway to the first of the dressed rooms, the

scullery. This has a fireplace with a cast-iron grate, a small boiler and a built-in sink under the window. The miniature kitchen range was made in Germany and is equipped with 13 accessories, including an axe and spit roast. A dresser holds the dinner service used during the queen's lifetime. Inside one of the cupboards Princess Louise left her signature, dated 1858.

In the adjoining kitchen is a scaled-down mid 19th-century Belgian range of the latest design and a chafing oven. The kitchen is well equipped, with all the utensils the children would have needed to prepare cakes, pastries and light meals.

Queen's Room, Lobby, Dressing Room and Sitting Room

The first floor is reached via external stairs and a balcony. The children often served luncheon or tea to their parents and other visitors in the dining room, known as the Queen's Room, as Victoria often worked here on her letters and State papers. She used the writing desk on which are displayed quills, headed writing paper, a blotting book and a silver seal stamped 'Swiss Cottage'.

Most of the furniture on this floor was made in England, including the remarkable American birch set of dining table (with five extra leaves in a stand), chairs with bobbin-turned legs, and fire screen, made for the cottage by the local Newport firm of Francis Pittis in 1854. An octagonal work table has a silver label stating that it was designed by the King of the Sandwich Islands and given by his widow, Emma, to Queen Victoria.

In the lobby are two cloak stands, a wardrobe, washstand and mirror, all by Pittis. In the dressing room on the left is a cane-seated couch, also by Pittis, upon which lies a gardening smock of one of the children. The ornate secretaire was made in Switzerland by Michael Leonz Wetli and bought at the Great Exhibition, probably for the cottage.

Initially the sitting room housed the children's museum. It contains a remarkable model shop, named 'Spratt, Grocer to her Majesty', used by the children to practise keeping accounts that were then checked for accuracy by Prince Albert.

Above: Clothes of the Bulgarian orphans rescued during the Crimean War
Right: The museum, showing the original cases
Below: Albert Barracks, probably built at the suggestion of Prince Albert, who used to play in a miniature fort at the Schloss Rosenau with his brother

SWISS COTTAGE MUSEUM

The museum was built in 1862 to house the collections that had outgrown the Swiss Cottage. It is also timber, but with a slate roof, and lacks the elaborate detailing of the cottage. The cases are original, but Sir Guy Laking (keeper of the king's armoury and curator of the Museum of London) rearranged the contents in 1916, and his distinctive gold labels remain.

Geological specimens (cases 21–30, 34–39), shells (42) – many from Osborne Beach – and stuffed animals and birds (31–33, 40–41) are on display, as are mementos of foreign tours, including antiquities (3–8) and rare items from the North American Micmac Indians (9), acquired by Bertie and Affie on separate tours in 1860 and 1869.

Case 12 contains the clothes of two Bulgarian orphans, Johnny (aged four) and Georgy (aged 15 months), who were rescued in 1854 by the British Navy after being wounded by the Turks in the Crimean War. Victoria took pity on the boys, who were brought up by Ann Jackman, wife of a carter at Osborne, in one of the Barton cottages.

VICTORIA FORT AND ALBERT BARRACKS

The miniature earth fort with redoubts near the museum was built against the political backdrop of the Crimean War, which broke out in March 1854, and ended on 30 March 1856, with the signing of the Treaty of Paris.

The appalling conditions endured by the British soldiers as reported in *The Times* caused a public outcry that eventually led to a number of nurses (headed by Florence Nightingale) being sent to the hospital at Scutari. Victoria Fort was completed in

1856, within two months of the Treaty of Paris. Bertie and Affie helped build it as a birthday surprise for the queen under the direction of Affie's governor, Lieutenant Cowell of the Royal Engineers, who had served in the Crimean War.

The brick-built Albert Barracks was added inside the fort in 1860, with the help of the 10-year-old Arthur, later Field Marshal the Duke of Connaught; a drawbridge was added in 1861.

OSBORNE BEACH

The wooded valley walk leads down from the broad walk to Osborne Beach. A private landing place was one of the main attractions of Osborne to the royal couple. In 1855 they added a landing house and 250m jetty (not English Heritage). The beach was much loved by the royal children; here they collected shells or dug in the sand with their governess, Lady Lyttelton. A tent was pitched each year on the shore to give them shelter. The alcove seat, decorated with blue Minton tiles, was built in 1869. Victoria often sat here to sketch or write.

After the queen's death in 1901 the beach was used by the convalescent home, which built the beach pavilion (now the café). During the Second World War, Canadian troops practised here for the D-Day landings; the remains of a Mulberry harbour (temporary harbour devised during the war to offload cargo on the Normandy beaches)

are visible at low tide further along the beach. The bay has become a haven for wildlife, with strips of vegetated shingle on the beach and eelgrass beds offshore that are of European significance.

Queen Victoria's Bathing Machine

Prince Albert was a firm believer in the benefits of sea bathing and the nearby beach was significant in his choice of Osborne. Beyond the alcove seat are the remains of the stone rails down which the queen's bathing machine ran into the sea from a covered recess which housed it and the floating bath when not in use. After her death the bathing machine was used as a chicken shed. It was moved in 1927, restored in the 1950s, and returned to the beach in 2012.

The children learnt to swim in a floating bath apparently devised by Albert, and built in 1854 by John and Robert White of Cowes. A wood grating held between two pontoons was raised or lowered according to the height of the swimmer. Because of the 4m tidal range, it was moored 60m out to sea and reached by a small boat manned by a pair of sailors from the royal yacht. Albert frequently took the older princes for a daily swim, while some of the princesses were taught by Eugene Loby, a young woman from Boulogne. The floating bath was broken up by a storm in 1900 but the model for it survives.

'Drove down to the beach with my maids and went into the bathing machine, where I undressed and bathed in the sea (for the first time in my life), a very nice bathing woman attending me. I thought it delightful till I put my head under the water, when I thought I should be stifled.' Victoria (above, in 1843, by Winterhalter) writing in her journal on 30 July 1847

Left: Victoria's bathing machine repositioned on sections of its original stone rails at Osborne Beach

History of the House

The house and estate created by Queen Victoria and Prince Albert at Osborne are unrivalled in terms of the intimate insight they can give into their private lives. The story of a marriage, a family and an empire is told in the richly decorated rooms and the treasures they contain. The tranquil gardens and wider landscape were vitally important for a couple seeking an escape from court life.

OSBORNE HOUSE

When Queen Victoria married Prince Albert of Saxe-Coburg in 1840, she had three palaces to live in: Windsor Castle, Buckingham Palace and the Royal Pavilion at Brighton. These soon proved unsuitable to the parents of a growing family, so in October 1843 the couple sought a country house. They wanted, to use the queen's words, 'a place of one's own, quiet and retired'.

The queen knew and liked the Isle of Wight, and the expanding railway network would enable her and Prince Albert to journey to the island from Buckingham Palace or Windsor in under four hours. The prime minister, Sir Robert Peel, sympathetically promoted her enquiries, which led

her to the Osborne estate. The couple visited Osborne in 1844. The queen wrote: 'It is impossible to imagine a prettier spot – we have a charming beach quite to ourselves – we can walk anywhere without being followed or mobbed.'

The old Osborne House was of brick and stone, of three storeys with a canted bay overlooking the Solent. It had been remodelled from an earlier house by 'Mr Sanderson' (probably the London architect John Sanderson) who in August 1774 supplied a plan for alterations to the then owner, Robert Pope Blachford (1742–90). Blachford's brick-walled kitchen garden to the west and brick stable block to the south survive, but all that remains of the 1770s house is the Portland stone porch, re-sited in about 1850 as a grand entrance to the 1770s kitchen garden.

In 1844 the queen wrote, 'I am delighted with the house, all over which we went. The rooms are small but very nice. With some few alterations and additions for the children it might be made an excellent home.' The queen sought *Gemütlichkeit* ('snugness' or 'cosiness'), but the lack of space she identified was a major problem and more extensive building works would be required.

Above: Old Osborne House, by C R Stanley, 1844

Below: Engraving of Thomas Cubitt, from a painting by H W Pickersgill (1782–1875)

Facing page: Prince Albert in the uniform of a colonel of the Rifle Brigade, by F X Winterhalter, 1859

Albert, who once complained that he was 'the husband not master of the house', recognized that Osborne would enable him to indulge some of his many passions: estate management, agricultural improvement, building, landscape design, gardening and education. It is clear from Victoria's journal that Albert was heavily involved with all aspects creating the new house and estate – in 1848 she referred to him as 'Albert the Creator'.

The queen bought the estate in May 1845 using her privy purse for the bargain price of a little under £28,000. Thomas Cubitt, the London builder and developer of entire suburbs in Pimlico, Bloomsbury and Belgravia, was engaged – 'such an honest, kind, good man', noted the queen.

Cubitt provided drawings and supervised the work. Much of the joinery and cast iron was manufactured in his London workshops. Bricks were made on the estate and the whole building was rendered with local Medina cement, the top coat coloured to imitate warm Bath stone. The exterior restoration by English Heritage replicates the original colour.

The Pavilion was the first part to be built, and the family moved in in September 1846. Cubitt's workmen did not undertake any 'gilding or fancy

painting' and he often left the rooms with green 'builder's finish' on the walls – a distemper that could be washed off later. Much of the Italian *cinquecento*-style internal decoration was designed under the guidance of Professor Ludwig Gruner of Dresden (1801–82), who had been appointed the queen's 'adviser in art' in 1845. He was an authority on Raphael and Italian frescos. The couple were pleased with the Italian effect. During the hot summer of 1852, the queen described the 'calm deep blue sea, the balmy air, all quite Italian'.

The design had considerable influence in Britain and elsewhere; for example, the Italianate design of Government House in Melbourne, Australia, built in the 1870s, shares many features with Osborne, including a prominent flag tower.

THE ESTATE

To make the estate viable more land was acquired, including the adjacent 500-acre Barton Manor, bought from Winchester College to serve as the home farm. Barton Manor (now privately owned) dated from the early 17th century, although built on the site of an Augustinian oratory founded in 1275. By 1864 the total landholding of Osborne rose to more than 2,000 acres.

Albert concerned himself with every aspect of the estate. In his own words, in February 1847, he was 'partly forrester, partly builder, partly farmer and partly gardener'. He wrote of his enthusiasm in the winter of 1859 to Vicky, now married to Prince Frederick William of Prussia: 'We had a fall of nine inches of snow, which looked wonderfully beautiful. I have all but broken my arms against the trees and shrubs, in clearing them, with poles, of the snow, which would otherwise have wholly crushed the fine evergreens and threatens to make havoc with the cypresses especially.'

Albert laid out the drives and paths, for privacy adding bends in the main drives to hide the house. A circular carriage ride ran near the perimeter of the estate. Here the couple often rode in a post-chaise. Charabancs were used when the family or visitors were given a tour of the park.

Barton Manor, the biggest farm, became a model of the latest agricultural methods. Cubitt fully 'restored' the manor house and reorganized its outbuildings as a model farm to supply Osborne

with daily produce. Farm machinery was harnessed to a portable steam engine. Awkward fields on the estate were squared off and new roads laid out. To improve the soil Albert and the estate bailiff or steward, Andrew Toward, laid under-draining using pipe tiles which, in the 1840s, were increasingly mass-produced. By 1864 they had laid over 360 miles of drains at an average depth of 4ft (1.2m).

Albert's interests in technology, economy, and environmentally friendly estate management came together with his experiments in designing and building a brick-lined gravity tank to turn sewage into farm manure by filtering it through clay, sand and charcoal. From 1850 he worked with the chemist Dr Lyon Playfair (1818–98), and that year he read a paper on the subject to the Royal Agricultural Society. At Osborne the 30ft (9m) long tank was sited on the north side of the valley as it took a steep fall of land to work. Albert's invention was not as widely applicable as he would have wished, but the tank at Osborne remained in operation throughout the 19th century.

Right: A plan of the Osborne estate. The English Heritage boundary is in red, representing only a fraction of the 2,000 acres (810ha) bought by Queen Victoria

Facing page: An aerial view of the house and terrace gardens from the north-east

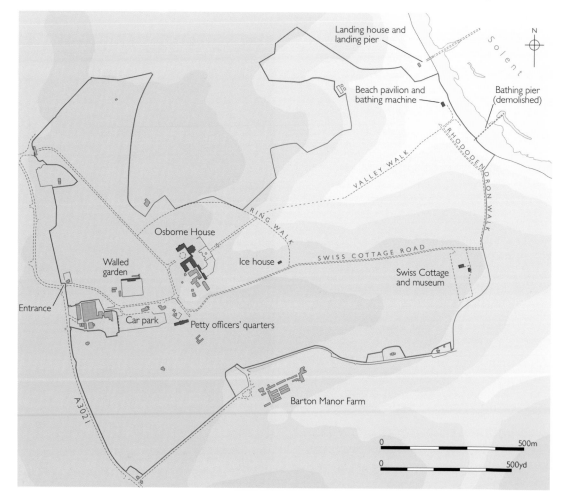

Below: Queen Victoria and her family by F X Winterhalter, 1847. In 1901 the original was sent to Buckingham Palace and a copy inserted in the frame in the dining room

Facing page: Family tree showing photographs of Victoria and Albert and their nine chidlren, all taken by John Jabez Edwin Mayall between 1860 and 1861

THE FAMILY

The royal family took delight in their seaside home and each year spent as much time as possible here and at Balmoral. Victoria spent a record total of 123 days at Osborne in 1848, when building and planting activity was at its height. The family, accompanied by the Court, established a regular pattern of visits by 1850, generally including four main periods at Osborne: in March, May, part of July and August, and from late November to just before Christmas, when they left for Windsor.

Hot summer days and the queen's liking for fresh air encouraged a routine which included breakfasting outside as often as possible. Both the queen and prince enjoyed walking and riding in the park, and it was rare for them to stay indoors all day. Victoria's references in her journal to reading and writing under the trees or in a small tent, taking tea in the summer house or with the children (see pages 44–5) at the Swiss Cottage, and Albert planting or visiting Barton Farm, conceal the daily stream of dispatch-boxes and papers.

The couple also hosted many royal visits at Osborne. Most were relations in some form, so they were largely family affairs. Of the remainder, the most successful visit was that of the Emperor and Empress of France, Napoleon III and Eugénie, in August 1857, which was informal to a degree that would have been impossible in London or Windsor, but in diplomatic terms it helped to cement the alliance between the two countries following the Crimean War. Personally, the queen was particularly captivated by the empress, and they remained close friends thereafter.

The Royal Family Tree

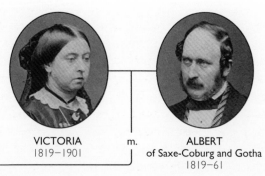

VICTORIA
1819–1901

m.

ALBERT
of Saxe-Coburg and Gotha
1819–61

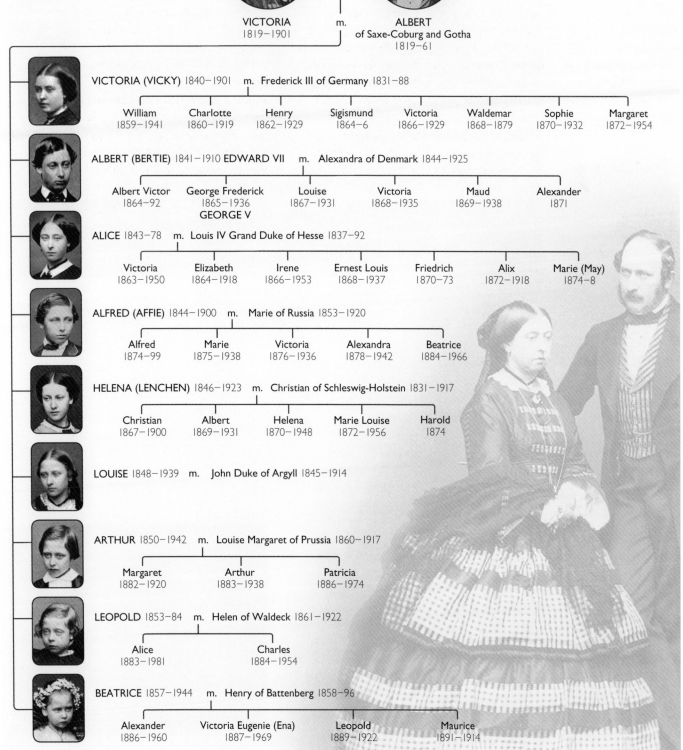

VICTORIA (VICKY) 1840–1901   m. Frederick III of Germany 1831–88

| William 1859–1941 | Charlotte 1860–1919 | Henry 1862–1929 | Sigismund 1864–6 | Victoria 1866–1929 | Waldemar 1868–1879 | Sophie 1870–1932 | Margaret 1872–1954 |

ALBERT (BERTIE) 1841–1910 EDWARD VII   m.   Alexandra of Denmark 1844–1925

| Albert Victor 1864–92 | George Frederick 1865–1936 GEORGE V | Louise 1867–1931 | Victoria 1868–1935 | Maud 1869–1938 | Alexander 1871 |

ALICE 1843–78   m. Louis IV Grand Duke of Hesse 1837–92

| Victoria 1863–1950 | Elizabeth 1864–1918 | Irene 1866–1953 | Ernest Louis 1868–1937 | Friedrich 1870–73 | Alix 1872–1918 | Marie (May) 1874–8 |

ALFRED (AFFIE) 1844–1900   m.   Marie of Russia 1853–1920

| Alfred 1874–99 | Marie 1875–1938 | Victoria 1876–1936 | Alexandra 1878–1942 | Beatrice 1884–1966 |

HELENA (LENCHEN) 1846–1923   m.   Christian of Schleswig-Holstein 1831–1917

| Christian 1867–1900 | Albert 1869–1931 | Helena 1870–1948 | Marie Louise 1872–1956 | Harold 1874 |

LOUISE 1848–1939   m.   John Duke of Argyll 1845–1914

ARTHUR 1850–1942   m.   Louise Margaret of Prussia 1860–1917

| Margaret 1882–1920 | Arthur 1883–1938 | Patricia 1886–1974 |

LEOPOLD 1853–84   m.   Helen of Waldeck 1861–1922

| Alice 1883–1981 | Charles 1884–1954 |

BEATRICE 1857–1944   m.   Henry of Battenberg 1858–96

| Alexander 1886–1960 | Victoria Eugenie (Ena) 1887–1969 | Leopold 1889–1922 | Maurice 1891–1914 |

Right: The children enacting a
tableau of the four seasons as
a surprise for Victoria and
Albert on their 10th wedding
anniversary at Windsor Castle,
10 February 1854, by Roger
Fenton (1819–69). From left:
Alice as Spring, Arthur and
Vicky as Summer, Helena as
the spirit of the Empress
Helena, Alfred as Autumn,
Louise and Bertie as Winter
Below right: A photograph
taken in August 1853 by
Ernst Becker. From left: Vicky
and Bertie holding butterfly
nets, Alice and Affie, on the
lower terrace at Osborne
Below: Sketches from Queen
Victoria's album of Vicky (top)
in 1842, Alfred in 1847 and
Helena (bottom) in 1848

The Royal Children

The relatively relaxed atmosphere at Osborne
allowed Victoria and Albert to spend more time with
their children than when in London or Windsor.
During the day, the queen would often hear them
recite French or help them with other lessons, and
most evenings they would visit her in the sitting room
in rotation, starting with the youngest. Prince Albert
delighted in being with his children and the queen's
journal frequently refers to his activities with them:
giving them a magic lantern show, showing them how
to catch butterflies, flying kites, or demonstrating
somersaults in the hay. Winter attractions included
ice-skating on the pond near Barton Farm or helping
the children to make snowmen.

Vicky (1840–1901), the Princess Royal, was a
precocious, talented child and her father's favourite.
Prince Albert produced many sketches of her at play
in the nursery and she thrived under his rigorous
educational regime. Vicky was married shortly after
her 17th birthday and thereafter lived in Berlin.

Unlike his sister, Bertie (1841–1910), the Prince
of Wales, showed little aptitude for his studies, fell
behind his younger siblings in his lessons and

developed a stammer and a temper. His relationship
with his parents was difficult, but to his sister Alice he
was particularly close.

Alice (1843–78) was a peacemaker, and alone
capable of persuading Bertie to partake in their
childhood games. After her early death, at the age
of 34, which came as a particular blow to Bertie, her
sister Helena described her as a 'loving Daughter and
Sister, the devoted Wife and Mother, and a perfect,
true Woman'. Next came Alfred (1844–1900), 'Affie',
an adventurous child who left home to join the Royal
Navy when he was 14. Affie was good with his hands,

delighting in taking apart and reassembling mechanical objects. He made toys for the other children, and he built a working steam engine and a musical box that could play *Rule Britannia*.

The next two children were Helena (1846–1923) and Louise (1848–1939). They had quite different temperaments and as they grew older often quarrelled. Helena, known as 'Lenchen', the German shortening of her name, was a tomboy, happiest mucking out the stables or digging her garden plot at the Swiss Cottage. She was known to punch her brothers on the nose when teased. She was closest to Affie, sharing his interest in boats and machinery.

Louise was deemed by the queen the prettiest of her daughters. She was strong-willed and a talented painter, and went on to study at the National Art Training School in Kensington and to have a sculpture studio at Osborne. Writing later about her happy childhood, she recalled dashing down to the Swiss Cottage garden to pick and eat the ripe gooseberries, strawberries and fresh green peas.

Good, obedient Arthur (1850–1942) was the queen's favourite. He was destined for a career in the Army, and on his first birthday announced 'Arta is going to be a soldier'. He could often be found

dressed in his Grenadier Guards' uniform acting out battles with his toy soldiers at Victoria Fort. His younger brother Leopold (1853–84) was the queen's 'child of anxiety', over whom she was fiercely protective. A mischievous child, but delicate, having inherited the disease haemophilia through his mother, any fall was liable to confine him to bed for days. It was after such a fall that he died, when only 30.

The last of the nine children was Beatrice (1857–1944), known affectionately as 'Baby'. She had in many ways a sad and solitary childhood, growing up in the aftermath of Prince Albert's death. But she was more indulged than her siblings and could be naughty. In the summer of 1862 she shut her governess in the barracks at Victoria Fort and demanded that she bark like a dog to be released.

The Swiss Cottage was the children's favourite place at Osborne. Here they grew fruit and vegetables, played at the miniature fort, cooked, entertained their parents, and collected objects for their expanding museum. This was all part of Prince Albert's educational strategy, with its emphasis on purposeful play and activities that taught the value of hard work, self-reliance and economy. The children revelled in this miniature world. Alice later commented that her childhood times at the Swiss Cottage had been the happiest of her life: 'no children' she said, 'ever were so happy, so spoilt with all the comforts and enjoyments that children could wish for, as we were.'

Top left: A sketch by Queen Victoria of (from left) Helena, Alice, Alfred, Louise, Bertie and Vicky enacting a scene from the play Die Tafel Birnen *in February 1853*
Left: Bertie and Alfred catching butterflies in the gardens at Osborne, June 1850, by Queen Victoria
Below: The family near the orangery on 26 May 1857 photographed by Leonida Caldesi (1822–91). From left: Alfred, 12; Prince Albert, 37; Helena, 11; Arthur, 7; Alice, 14; Beatrice, 6 weeks; Queen Victoria, 38; Vicky, 16; Louise, 9; Leopold, 4; Bertie, 15

Above: Osborne 1865, or
Sorrow, by Sir Edwin
Landseer, which hangs in the
horn room. All the figures sat
for Landseer in 1865, but he
also used photographs taken
at Osborne to aid his
composition. The painting was
not begun until 1867. The
queen, in deep mourning, sits
on her pony Flora, held by
John Brown. Louise and
Helena sit on a bench
wearing lilac half-mourning

The Death of Albert

The prince's constitution was frail and he
constantly drove himself too hard. Writing to his
eldest daughter, Vicky, the Empress of Prussia, in
1859, he complained wearily of the 'treadmill of
never-ending business. The donkey in Carisbrooke,
which you remember, is my true counterpart. He,
too, would rather munch thistles in the Castle
Moat, than turn round in the wheel at the Castle
Well; and small are the thanks he gets for his
labours.' For Victoria 1861 was a devastating year.
Her mother died in March, and the year ended
with the increasing illness and finally the death of
the Prince Consort – officially from typhoid – at
Windsor on 14 December.

The widowed queen was overwhelmed with
grief and immediately retreated to Osborne,
supported by all her daughters (apart from Vicky
who was confined in Berlin). Her uncle Leopold,
King of the Belgians, met her there, as did Albert's
brother, Duke Ernest from Coburg. As the
dispatch boxes mounted, Arthur Helps, the privy
council secretary, summoned a privy council
meeting on 6 January 1862. The queen did not

see her ministers, who 'were in dear Albert's
room, & I in mine with the door open.'

The queen remained at Osborne until early
March 1862. She never ceased to mourn. She
generally wore black, with a white widow's cap,
and her writing paper and envelopes were thickly
bordered with black. The prince's influence
governed much of her later life. As she wrote in
December 1861, 'His wishes – his plans – about
everything, his views about every thing are to be
my law! And no human power will make me
swerve from what he decided and wished.'

The queen's annual routine changed, however,
as she appears to have avoided the associations of
earlier anniversaries. She generally returned to
Osborne in mid December after visiting Albert's
mausoleum at Frogmore. Her stay at Osborne
now included Christmas, but never her birthday
on 24 May, which was almost invariably spent at
Balmoral, as was Albert's birthday in August.
Conversely, her wedding anniversary, formerly
celebrated at Buckingham Palace or Windsor, was
subsequently observed at Osborne almost every
year for the rest of her life.

THE LATER YEARS

The daily running of the queen's affairs required a considerable amount of assistance. Her principal dresser, Miss Marianne Skerrett, who entered service in 1837, was also her confidante. After the death of Albert, Princess Alice and, later, Princess Beatrice partially fulfilled that role. Beatrice, the queen's youngest daughter, became her constant companion, remaining with her family in the Durbar wing after the early death of her husband, Prince Henry of Battenberg, in 1896.

Sir Henry Ponsonby (1825–95) was the most prominent of the queen's private secretaries, Albert having fulfilled this role until his death. Ponsonby was appointed equerry to Prince Albert in 1856, and to the queen in 1861. In 1870 he became her private secretary, and from 1878 keeper of the privy purse as well. His diplomacy made him an indispensable link between the queen and her ministers, and even her children.

Ponsonby died on the estate in 1895 and is buried in St Mildred's, Whippingham. Arthur Ponsonby (1871–1946), his third son and his biographer, commented, 'From my birth until his death my father seemed always to be writing and never have any holidays.' But Ponsonby's diaries do not harp on the constant demands made on him; instead, they are scattered with references to playing croquet in summer, and skating and ice hockey in winter with the royal princesses. An eye had to be kept out for the queen, who apparently disapproved of ice hockey. If her outrider in livery

and top hat was spotted, the sticks were hurriedly thrown into the bank and the whole company turned innocently to figure-skating.

Victoria was renowned for her imperviousness to the cold. Lord Clarendon (1800–70), several times foreign secretary, visited Osborne in 1860 and complained of the queen playing the 'royal game of summer worse than ever – all the windows were open and all the noses were blue at and after dinner last night, and today, tho' people are shivering, the Queen I understand doubts whether it is not too hot to drive to Freshwater.' Cubitt's heating system provided background warmth, but it also relied on fires in

Above: Victoria at Frogmore working outside with one of her Indian servants in attendance. She used a similar tent at Osborne

Below: The queen and some of her family at Osborne, 1898. Left to right: Prince Leopold of Battenberg, Princess Aribert of Anhalt, Duchess of York with Prince Edward and Princess Mary (on knee), Princess Margaret of Connaught, Prince Alexander of Battenberg (on ground), Duke of York with Prince Albert, Queen Victoria, Prince Arthur of Connaught, Duchess of Connaught, Princess Patricia of Connaught (on ground), Princess Henry of Battenberg, Princess Ena of Battenberg, Princess Helena Victoria of Schleswig-Holstein, Prince Maurice of Battenberg

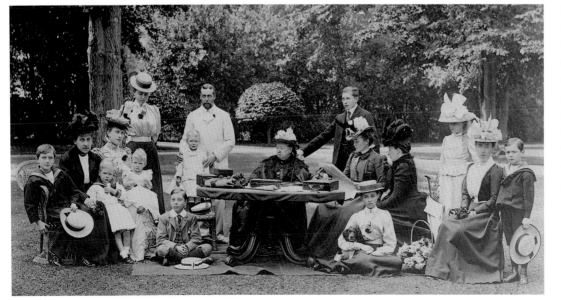

Right: *Watercolour of Queen Victoria on her deathbed, 24 January 1901, by Hubert von Herkomer (1849–1914). The artist was commissioned by a newspaper and given permission by the king to make the drawing. The queen, draped with white lace, wore her wedding veil and held the tortoiseshell cross which formerly hung above her bed. The bed was strewn with lilies, which gave a strong scent to the room*

the rooms. The queen preferred to burn beech logs and had a dislike of coal. (Even Albert, writing to his eldest daughter one morning in September 1858, confessed, 'Osborne is green and beautiful, but the weather cold and stormy. Mama will be much hurt when she gets up and finds I have had a fire lit.') Marie Mallett, a lady-in-waiting, wrote in January 1891: 'The house is fairly warm, but the Drawing Room so "Siberian" and I came to bed chilled to the bone.'

Some evenings were enlivened by lectures, recitals or theatricals, which the queen termed 'treats'. In 1866 the pianist Hallé stayed to play for the queen. Others who performed at Osborne included Signor Tosti, Dame Clara Butt and Dame Nellie Melba, and theatrical performances were given by Henry Irving and Ellen Terry.

The early practice of performing *tableaux vivants* over the New Year was revived some time after the death of the Prince Consort. A biblical tableau of Naomi and Ruth in 1888 was described by the queen as 'not quite so successful as it might have been, owing to the ladies getting the giggles and shaking'.

THE DEATH OF QUEEN VICTORIA

Even in the 1890s Queen Victoria stayed at Osborne for 90 to 100 days each year, continuing the daily routine established for over 50 years. She remained alert, but her eyesight was failing and Sir Henry Ponsonby was urged to write larger, and use blacker ink. A combination of rheumatism and two bad falls meant she was often pushed in her 'rolling chair'.

By 1900 she was dozing during the day, and failing to sleep at night. Her first diary entry for 1901 recorded, 'Another year begun & I am feeling so weak & unwell that I enter upon it sadly.'

On 17 January 1901 the queen suffered a slight stroke. Members of the family started to arrive at Osborne, and soon every bed was occupied. She was nursed in her bedroom, but on 22 January, surrounded by her family, which included the future Edward VII and Kaiser Wilhelm II of Germany, the 81-year-old Queen of Great Britain and Ireland and Empress of India died. The Duke of Argyll described the queen's last moments as 'like a great three-decker ship sinking. She kept on rallying then sinking'.

The calm within the Pavilion contrasted with the clamour outside the gates, where reporters waited to telegraph the news across the world. Frederick Ponsonby (1867–1935), Henry's second son, recalled: 'The scene on the hill down to Cowes was disgraceful. Reporters in carriages and on bicycles were seen racing for the post office in East Cowes, and men were shouting as they ran, "The queen is dead".' It was the end of an era.

Frederick Ponsonby described the dining room, where the queen lay in state, which 'was hung round with curtains and draperies. The coffin was covered with crimson velvet and ermine with the crown in diamonds on a cushion, and the Order of the Garter which the queen had worn on a raised platform covered by the Royal Standard. The room was lighted by eight huge candles and there were palms around the room in addition to the masses of wreaths. It was all gorgeous with colour and most impressive.'

The coffin was guarded by four men from Queen's Company, Grenadier Guards, in scarlet tunics standing with reversed arms, one at each corner, plus a member of the household at the foot of the coffin. On 1 February the coffin,

draped with a white satin pall embroidered by the Royal School of Needlework founded by Princess Helena, with a gold cross in the middle and the royal arms in the corners, was carried from the house by sailors from the royal yacht, and placed on the gun carriage. The whole cortège moved slowly through East Cowes to Trinity Pier where the coffin was placed on the royal yacht *Alberta*.

Above: Queen Victoria's coffin lying in state at Osborne, with Grenadier Guardsmen and one of the Queen's Indian attendants standing guard, by Amédée Forestier (1854–1930), 1901

Below: The queen's funeral procession leaves Osborne, 1 February 1901

The small yacht, accompanied by the *Victoria and Albert* and the *Osborne*, was dwarfed between the battleships and cruisers anchored in two lines all the way to Portsmouth. The queen forbade black for her funeral, and the streets of London were hung with purple, tied with white silk bows. Her coffin, still draped with the white and gold pall, was laid to rest alongside Albert's in the royal mausoleum at Frogmore, Windsor.

OSBORNE IN THE 20TH CENTURY

The death of Queen Victoria at Osborne in 1901 left a vacuum much more dramatic in its consequences for the estate than the death of Albert, its creator. The land and outlying buildings were gradually disposed of.

Osborne was the private possession of the royal family but Edward VII did not need it: Sandringham was more convenient and Barton Manor was enough for overspill accommodation during Cowes Week (Barton was sold in 1922). Only four of Edward's eight siblings were still alive, and Beatrice was the only one to retain a home in the Isle of Wight, but she preferred to live in Osborne Cottage. Beatrice was also governess of the Isle of Wight and of Carisbrooke Castle, and from 1914 made the governor's residence at Carisbrooke Castle (now English Heritage) her

summer home. The queen had bequeathed her private journals to Beatrice, with the injunction that she was to modify portions which she considered unsuitable for preservation. Beatrice copied out an edited version, burning the original volume as each year was completed.

On coronation day 1902 King Edward VII wrote: 'As Osborne is sacred to the memory of the late Queen, it is the King's wish that … His People shall always have access to the House which must forever be associated with Her beloved name.' A committee appointed by the king determined in December 1902 that a convalescent home for officers should be established in part of the house, and the stables used for naval cadets. These principles were enshrined in the 1902 Osborne Estate Act.

The Royal Naval College, Osborne

The college was established in the grounds in 1903 for the training of officer cadets as a result of reforms leading to a rapid expansion of the Navy. Boys arrived at the age of 13 and stayed for two years before moving to Britannia Royal Naval College at Dartmouth. Building began in March 1903 to the designs of Henry Nicholas Hawks (1855–1911), architect to the Office of Works, and it was opened by Edward VII the following August.

The first intake was 72, but within two years the number had risen to 400, increasing to its maximum of 500 during the First World War.

The site included classrooms in the former stable block, dormitories (an eventual total of 12), civilian and officers' accommodation (the petty officers' quarters was adapted by English Heritage in 2006 as a reception centre), messing facilities, a training mast, gymnasiums and a cricket pavilion (now used as holiday lets). The new buildings were designed in an Office of Works version of the fashionable municipal Arts and Crafts style.

Both the future Edward VIII and his brother George VI attended as cadets. Their letters home were full of the usual boyish excitement for all that was going on – meeting the explorers Shackleton and Scott, performing in a pantomime, or

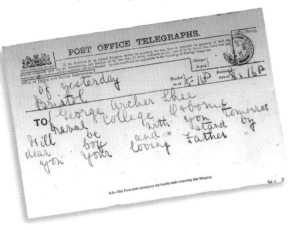

enthusing about the latest crazes. Today the college is remembered as the setting of the tragic Archer-Shee scandal of 1909, dramatized by Terence Rattigan in his play *The Winslow Boy*. George Archer-Shee, an Osborne cadet, was accused of stealing a five-shilling postal order, and his parents were asked to withdraw him from the Navy. They appealed, and the case went to court. He was finally vindicated to public jubilation, but his family were financially ruined. Having lost his Naval career, Archer-Shee enlisted in the Army in 1914 and was killed at Ypres, Belgium, within the first month of the war.

The college contributed to strengthening the Navy before the First World War, but by 1920 the Navy was over-manned, and the number of cadets at Osborne had fallen to about 50. In 1921 the college closed. In 1933 many of the buildings, such as the dormitories (on the site of the visitors' car park), were demolished.

The Convalescent Home

The Edward VII Convalescent Home for Officers serving in His Majesty's Forces was opened in 1904 within part of the main and household wings. It was run by the house governor, who also managed the royal apartments. Two- and three-room suites were converted into bedrooms and bathrooms by H N Hawks, architect to the Office of Works. Furniture was designed by Rowland Bailey of the Office of Works and made by Maples. The terraces were the preserve of the convalescents, and a nine-hole golf course was laid out for their use.

In the First World War officers were not allowed home to convalesce as it delayed their return to the Front; many were sent to Osborne. The poet and author Robert Graves described being at Osborne during the First World War, when A A Milne (later author of the Christopher Robin stories) was also a patient. Graves was president of the humorous Royal Albert Society. When he found on the beach a fender with frayed rope resembling hair, he dressed it up with wet clothes and draped it with seaweed before alerting the coastguard to the presence of a dead man on the beach. 'The coastguard stopped a few yards off, and exclaimed, holding his nose: "Pooh, don't he 'alf stink!" ' The hoax was reported in the paper.

No major alterations were made until the late 1980s, when it was effectively transformed into a nursing home. Escalating costs of patient care prompted its closure in 2000.

When he found on the beach a fender with frayed rope resembling hair, he dressed it up with wet clothes and a boot

Below: Cubitt's 1845 kitchens near the Georgian stables were modernized and used by the convalescent home until the 1950s, when they were converted into a garage

A Maid at Osborne

Domestics were only allowed to go to the kitchen if on an errand for matron, so we didn't get to know the kitchen staff

After leaving school at the age of 15 in 1955, Kathy Barter began work as a 'domestic' in the King Edward VII Convalescent Home for Officers, where she entered a household still run with Victorian discipline.

'Full-time maids were expected to live-in then, in a large dormitory. We did have a small room each, but we shared the bathrooms and toilets. I was the youngest and the 15th housemaid then. There were also six parlourmaids and the governor's maid living in our block. There was also the cooks' and kitchen-maids' dormitory. They didn't mix with us and had their own sitting and dining room.

'Domestics were only allowed to go to the kitchen if on an errand for matron, or sent by the supervisor, so we didn't get to know the kitchen staff well. Also, there was the men's dormitory for the valets, porters and others. Of course that was strictly out of bounds, and they also had their own sitting and dining room. Rules were very strict, and everything was more or less run on military lines.'

From Serving Life at Osborne 1955–2000, *by Kathy Barter*

Right: Kathy Barter in the uniform of a parlourmaid, carrying the pig bucket, 1965. 'You were never allowed a dirty apron, or to have your straps twisted'

OSBORNE TODAY

Edward VII did not want the public to have access to Queen Victoria's private rooms in the Pavilion, so the first floor was sealed by iron gates and preserved for over 50 years as a family shrine.

Other apartments were opened to the public free of charge, carpeting was stripped out and copies were substituted for some paintings. Major re-presentation schemes were also undertaken, notably the rearrangements of the Durbar Room and the Swiss Cottage and museum by Sir Guy Laking during the First World War. Nevertheless, Osborne retains much of its original contents, which are part of the Royal Collection.

The grounds were maintained by the Office of Works, but the Victorian planting was abandoned: at the Swiss Cottage shrubs and flowers replaced vegetables in the children's plots in about 1904 and the terrace parterres were simplified after the First World War. Osborne's fortunes reached a nadir in the early 1920s, when Victorian art and architecture were out of fashion, but thereafter visitor numbers (who now had to pay) increased.

In 1954 Elizabeth II gave permission for the gates to Queen Victoria's private apartments to be unlocked and the public admitted. In 1977 Queen Elizabeth's silver jubilee saw an upsurge in visitor numbers. Some rooms were redecorated, but detailed paint research does not appear to have begun until 1982 when the colour schemes of the Grand Corridor were analysed. Redecoration there was not complete until 1985.

In 1986 English Heritage took over the management of Osborne from the Department of the Environment. In cooperation with the Royal Collection, English Heritage is slowly re-presenting rooms by removing objects which have arrived since 1901 and replacing some that left Osborne earlier. It is seeking to re-emphasize the *raison-d'être* of the house as a family home.

Within the grounds, English Heritage has reinstated much of Albert's planting and woodland. The conservation of plants and the management of wildlife habitats and ecosystems are significant drivers for modern management of the Osborne estate. Large areas are maintained as wildflower and grass meadows for biodiversity. The estate is also a haven for protected species including red squirrels and buzzards, which are often seen above the valley from the Swiss Cottage road.